# The Peculiar Past in
# ANCIENT GREECE

by Charis Mather

BEARPORT
PUBLISHING

Minneapolis, Minnesota

## Credits

All images are courtesy of Shutterstock.com, unless otherwise specified. With thanks to Getty Images, Thinkstock Photo, and iStockphoto.
Cover – Macrovector, ONYXprj, NotionPic, Nsit, korinoxe, Perfect_kebab. 4–5 – English: Dietrich Reimer, Public domain, via Wikimedia Commons, Leo von Klenze, Public domain, via Wikimedia Commons, vkilikov, photo by Grant Mitchell, CC BY 2.0 <https://creativecommons. org/licenses/by/2.0>, via Wikimedia Commons, lemono, kamellys. 6–7 – Vectorfair, Walter Crane, Public domain, via Wikimedia Commons, See U in History, Edouard-Joseph Dantan, Public domain, via Wikimedia Commons, VasyaV, AnonymousUnknown author, Public domain, via Wikimedia Commons, VIATOR IMPERI from HISPANIA, CC BY-SA 2.0 <https:// creativecommons.org/licenses/by-sa/2.0>, via Wikimedia Commons, Maquiladora. 8–9 – R. Lemieszek, elmm, Palazzo Massimo alle Terme, CC BY 2.5 <https://creativecommons.org/ licenses/by/2.5>, via Wikimedia Commons, VasyaV, rizki dian pratama, HappyPictures. 10–11 – Sidhe, oxanaart, Georges Rochegrosse, Public domain, via Wikimedia Commons, Luc-Olivier Merson, Public domain, via Wikimedia Commons. 12–13 – Maso Finiguerra, Public domain, via Wikimedia Commons, Pranch, Top Vector Studio, muratart. 14–15 – Los Angeles County Museum of Art, Public domain, via Wikimedia Commons, Crescenzio Onofri, Public domain, via Wikimedia Commons, Chatree Puksri, Olesia Barhii, Claudia Pylinskaya. 16–17 – Lev Paraskevopoulos, Nicolas-André Monsiau (1754–1837), Public domain, via Wikimedia Commons, Macrovector, delcarmat, Gilmanshin. 18–19 – Apsaras, dominique landau, Andrii Bezvershenko, Nsit, A.B.G., Hoika Mikhail, grmarc. 20–21 – Abraham Janssens I, Public domain, via Wikimedia Commons, serato, GoodFocused, Jean-Léon Gérôme, Public domain, via Wikimedia Commons, Friedrich Georg Weitsch, Public domain, via Wikimedia Commons, Artmim. 22–23 – Henryk Siemiradzki, Public domain, via Wikimedia Commons, Sabelskaya, HappyPictures, Lefteris Papaulakis, NotionPic, ONYXprj, See page for author, CC BY 4.0 <https://creativecommons.org/licenses/by/4.0>, via Wikimedia Commons. 24–25 – M Selcuk Oner, NotionPic, Pong Wira, Ansis Klucis, Wellcome Images, CC BY 4.0 <https:// creativecommons.org/licenses/by/4.0>, via Wikimedia Commons, Photo: Alinari, CC0, via Wikimedia Commons, VectorShow. 26–27 – Unknown man, Internet Archive Book Images, No restrictions, via Wikimedia Commons, Viacheslav Lopatin, Jona Lendering, CC0, via Wikimedia Commons, Evgeniya Mokeeva. 28–29 – tan_tan, Eroshka, ABB Photo, NotionPic, anka77. 30 – Nathan Holland.

## Bearport Publishing Company Product Development Team

President: Jen Jenson; Director of Product Development: Spencer Brinker; Managing Editor: Allison Juda; Associate Editor: Naomi Reich; Associate Editor: Tiana Tran; Art Director: Colin O'Dea; Designer: Elena Klinkner; Designer: Kayla Eggert; Product Development Assistant: Owen Hamlin

Library of Congress Cataloging-in-Publication Data is available at www.loc.gov or upon request from the publisher.

ISBN: 979-8-88916-479-1 (hardcover)
ISBN: 979-8-88916-484-5 (paperback)
ISBN: 979-8-88916-488-3 (ebook)

For more information, write to Bearport Publishing, 5357 Penn Avenue South, Minneapolis, MN 55419.

# CONTENTS

# STRANGE TIME
## TO BE ALIVE!

About 2,500 years ago, the ancient Greeks were living ordinary lives along the Mediterranean coast. At least, everything seemed ordinary to them!

If you look back at the odd events and unusual people in ancient Greece, you realize what a peculiar past it was!

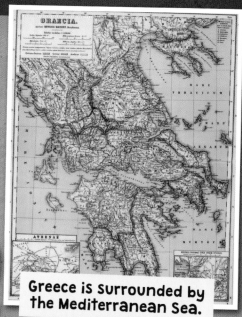

Greece is surrounded by the Mediterranean Sea.

Today, ancient Greece is remembered for its beautiful buildings, action-packed **myths**, and deep-thinking **philosophers**. However, if you look deeper, you'll see that ancient Greek history is a whole lot weirder than you first thought.

Ancient Greece was divided into areas called city-states, which were like mini countries. Life in each city-state was a little different. They each had their own rulers, laws, and armies. Unfortunately, these different parts of ancient Greece didn't always get along. Fighting often broke out between city-states.

# ANCIENT OLYMPICS

Although the ancient Greeks often fought, they would still put their wars on hold every four years for the Olympic Games. When this huge sporting event first started in ancient Greece, the top athletes competed for crowns made of olive leaves.

Today, Olympic athletes compete for medals, rather than leafy crowns.

What might win you a crown? There were many ancient Olympic events.

Foot racing

Wrestling

Discus throwing

Javelin throwing

Women were not allowed to join in the Olympics. But that didn't stop Princess Cynisca of Sparta from taking part. She paid a man to race her **chariot** horses, and he won. Because she owned the horses, Cynisca became the first female Olympic champion.

Chariot racing

What else wasn't allowed in these Olympics? Clothing! Athletes stripped down and covered their bodies in olive oil. After the events, their oily sweat was collected in bottles. Rich people bought this sweat believing it would make them as strong and healthy as the athletes. *Yuck!*

A strigil was used for scraping sweat off athletes.

ATHLETE SWEAT

# IN IT TO WIN IT

## FIGHTING FIT

Some ancient Greek sports were very violent. If you weren't willing to deal with lots of pain, the fighting events probably weren't for you. Unless you were Melankomas of Caria, that is. This boxer was famous for winning

fights without ever hitting the other person. Instead, he blocked or ducked every punch until the other athlete was worn out and gave up.

You win! I'm too tired!

An ancient Greek boxing match

## PAINFUL PANKRATION

The most brutal Greek sport was pankration, which was a combination of kickboxing and wrestling. Fighters were not allowed to bite or poke their opponents' eyes, but everything else was allowed—including breaking bones!

## A FIGHT TO THE FINISH

The athlete Arrhichion had one of the strangest pankration wins ever. He was losing but somehow managed to let loose one final kick before dropping dead. Arrhichion's kick was so powerful and painful that his opponent gave up. Arrhichion's dead body was declared the winner!

# A RUN TO REMEMBER

Olympic athletes were not the only ones famous for their fitness. Greek armies sometimes used super-speedy runners called hemerodromes to carry messages quickly over long distances. Hemerodromes were trained to run for days at a time with almost no rest.

One of the most famous hemerodromes was a runner named Pheidippides. He ran from Athens to Sparta to ask the Spartan army for help in a war against the Persians. The stories say that Pheidippides ran almost 150 miles (240 km) in just two days!

Marathon

Sparta

Athens

In the end, the Athenian army defeated the Persians during a battle at Marathon. However, there was still one important message to deliver.

The Battle of Marathon

## A MARATHON EFFORT

A runner named Eukles was ordered to carry the news of victory from the Marathon battlefield back to Athens. Eukles finished the run, passed on his message . . . and then passed away!

Eukles's famous run from Marathon to Athens inspired today's best-known long-distance race—the marathon.

# UNFORTUNATE ENDS

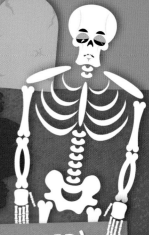

Some ancient Greeks, such as Arrhichion and Eukles, are remembered for their heroic deaths. Others died in ways that were simply absurd.

## THE TORTOISE AND THE HAIR(LESS HEAD)

Ancient Greek Aeschylus was famous for writing **tragic** plays. Little did he know his own life would come to a tragic end. A hungry eagle mistook his bald head for a rock. The eagle dropped a tortoise on Aeschylus's head, hoping to crack it open for a tasty snack. Instead, it caved in the playwright's skull!

Many ancient Greek stories have been retold so many times that it is hard to separate fact from **fiction**.

12

To show that you enjoyed a play or speech in an ancient Greek **theater**, you would throw your hat or coat at the performers. But this clothes-throwing could get out of hand. After giving an inspiring speech, the lawmaker Draco was smothered to death by all the clothing his fans threw at him. *Oops!*

A Greek theater

# THE DOWNSIDE OF BEING DEAD

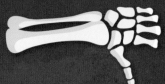

Ancient Greeks believed death was just the first part of a journey through the **underworld,** also known as Hades. Five very unpleasant and dangerous rivers ran through Hades.

A river in Hades

- The River Styx (the river of hatred)
- The Acheron (the river of misery)
- The Phlegethon (the river of blazing fire)
- The Cocytus (the river of wailing)
- The Lethe (the river of forgetfulness)

People believed the River Styx would melt anything that touched it—except things made of horse or donkey hooves!

## THE RIVER STYX

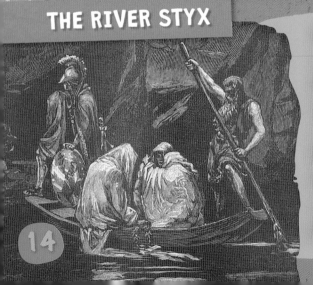

In order to get to the underworld, people believed that they needed to pay a **ferryman** to row them across the River Styx. Some ancient Greeks were buried with a coin in their mouth to pay the ferryman.

## THE THREE-HEADED DOG

Once someone was in the underworld, they could not get out again. The gates around Hades were guarded by Cerberus, a dog with three heads and snakes coming out of different parts of its body.

## DEAD IS DEAD . . . RIGHT?

Ancient Greeks were not convinced that the dead and buried would stay that way. Some bodies were held down by heavy rocks or jars to keep them from crawling out of their graves as **zombies**.

I wanted to rest in peace, not pieces.

15

# GRUESOME GODS

Zeus

Athena

Poseidon

Ares

Artemis

Ancient Greeks believed in 12 main gods who lived on the top of Mount Olympus. There were also many lesser gods.

Each god was in charge of different things. There were gods of earthquakes, thieves, poison, the underworld, and parties.

Hermes

Hera

Dionysus

Hephaestus

Demeter

Apollo

Aphrodite

There are very strange stories about some Greek gods.

## STONE-COLD CRONUS

Cronus was a god who happened to be an awful father. He was so afraid his kids would steal his power that he would swallow them whole as soon as they were born. Fed up with having her kids eaten, Cronus's wife, Rhea, hid her next child and fed Cronus a baby-sized rock instead. The **gullible** god gulped it right down.

The baby Rhea rescued was named Zeus. He grew up to save his swallowed siblings by making his dad vomit them back up!

Zeus

17

# SO MUCH DRAMA!

Ancient Greeks loved going to see plays. Most cities had at least one theater.

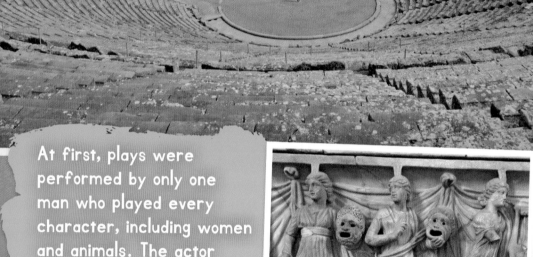

At first, plays were performed by only one man who played every character, including women and animals. The actor changed costumes and wore different masks to show who he was playing.

Sometimes, plays were performed as competitions. Audiences chose which play was the best. If your play got enough votes, you might become the winner and receive . . . a goat!

Audiences loved seeing different characters from myths come to life onstage. The plays could show funny stories called comedies or sad stories known as tragedies.

One tragedy told the story of Prometheus, who stole fire from Zeus and gave it to humans. As punishment, Zeus had him tied to a rock and sent an eagle to eat his liver every day. Prometheus's liver would grow back, only to be eaten again the next day!

# DEEP THINKERS

Ancient Greece was famous for its philosophers. These people spent all their time thinking about life and how best to live it. Some of their ideas could get a little wacky.

## A DOG'S DINNER

Heraclitus was a philosopher who believed he could treat an illness by covering himself in cow poop. Unfortunately, he ended up getting stuck in the stinky stuff. While struggling to escape the poop pile, Heraclitus was eaten by dogs!

# POTTY PHILOSOPHY

The philosopher Diogenes held beliefs that led to some interesting life choices. He made his home inside a large pot. Even stranger, Diogenes wasn't shy about peeing and pooping just about anywhere—even in the street or on a floor.

Diogenes did not show much respect to other people. Another famous philosopher named Plato once described humans as two-legged creatures without feathers. Diogenes made fun of Plato's definition by plucking all the feathers from a chicken and declaring it a human.

What did I do to deserve this?

Plato

Diogenes

# BAD MEDICINE

While a lot of ancient Greek ideas were good, many of the time's medical treatments would probably make you a whole lot sicker.

## TASTELESS TREATMENTS

Doctors in ancient Greece used their sense of taste to help them decide what was making people sick. It was common for doctors to nibble on a patient's earwax, snot, or even vomit!

## SACRED SLOBBER

Asklepios

The Greek god of medicine, Asklepios, was often shown with a dog or a snake. This led some people to believe they would be healed if they lay down in snake-filled temples or if they had their injuries licked by a **sacred** dog.

Luckily, the temple snakes were not **venomous!**

## CROCODILE DUNG CREAM

Ancient Greek doctors might have suggested rubbing cream made from crocodile poop around your eyes to make you look younger. This treatment didn't do much for your skin, but it sure did make you stinky!

Don't try any of these ancient treatments yourself!

23

# SHARING IS CARING

## POOPING IN PUBLIC

If you wanted to poop in ancient Greece, you may have had to do it in public. Public toilets were long benches with holes in them. You would do your business sitting right next to other people, with no stalls or walls for privacy.

Toilet paper didn't exist yet. Instead, people wiped with pebbles or bits of pottery. *Ouch!*

An open-air shower

# SHARED SHOWERS

Pooping wasn't the only bathroom activity that the ancient Greeks were happy to do in public. Showering was also often a group activity, and some showers were even out in the open!

How would you wash yourself like someone in ancient Greece?

STEP 1 Scrub your skin with clay, sand, ash, or a rough rock. There was no soap back then—sorry!

STEP 2 Rub oil onto your skin.

STEP 3 Scrape off all the grit and oil with a strigil (the same tool used to scrape athlete sweat).

STEP 4 Rinse off with water.

# GREEK GLAMOUR

If you wanted to fit in with the ancient Greek cool kids, you would have to keep up with the latest fashion trends.

## HIGHBROW FASHION

Some ancient Greeks believed having one eyebrow that stretched across the whole forehead made them look beautiful and clever. So, they joined their two eyebrows with makeup. If the eyebrow wasn't bushy enough, they sometimes added goat hair!

## LOOKING LOVELY

Some people powdered themselves with chalk or **lead** to look more like the creamy-skinned Greek goddess of love and beauty, Aphrodite.

Aphrodite

Lead is **toxic**. Poisoning from this metal can lead to stomach pain, confusion, weakness, organ damage, and death.

# TATTOO TABOO

**This isn't a tattoo, I swear! My pen just exploded!**

**Tattoos** are fashionable today, but in ancient Greece they were *not* cool at all! They were usually given to criminals as a form of punishment. Unless you wanted to show off that you'd broken the law, you probably would want to cover those tats up.

When the ancient Athenian and Samian armies went to war, both sides gave tattoos to their prisoners. Athenian prisoners got tattoos of a Samian ship, and Samian prisoners got tattoos of an Athenian owl.

A Samian soldier

27

# SAVAGE SPARTANS

Boys growing up in the city-state of Sparta were expected to be soldiers. To toughen them up for the army, Spartan boys were not given much to eat. They were expected to steal food if they were hungry. When they were seven, they were sent off to war school.

Spartan girls did not go to war school, but they had to be tough, too. They learned how to wrestle and throw javelins.

I'm not scared! What makes you think I'm scared?

Bravery was very important to the Spartans. One odd way that warriors showed they weren't afraid of dying was by brushing their hair before a battle. If a warrior showed fear, other soldiers would shave off half his beard!

The Spartans taught children about being tough by telling them this nasty little story:

One day, a young Spartan boy stole a fox. The fox's owners noticed that the animal was missing and went searching for it. The boy tucked the fox under his shirt to hide it.

Spartan boys were encouraged to steal. However, if they were caught, they were punished for not being sneaky enough!

While the owners questioned the boy, the fox began to bite through the thief's skin. Not wanting to be caught, the boy didn't cry or show any pain on his face. The boy's toughness saved him from the **shame** of being caught.

# SERIOUSLY STRANGE

The peculiar past in ancient Greece could be seriously strange. From naked sporting events and public pooping to wild warriors and wacky philosophers, ancient Greece had some terrible tales, surprising stories, and hard-to-believe history!

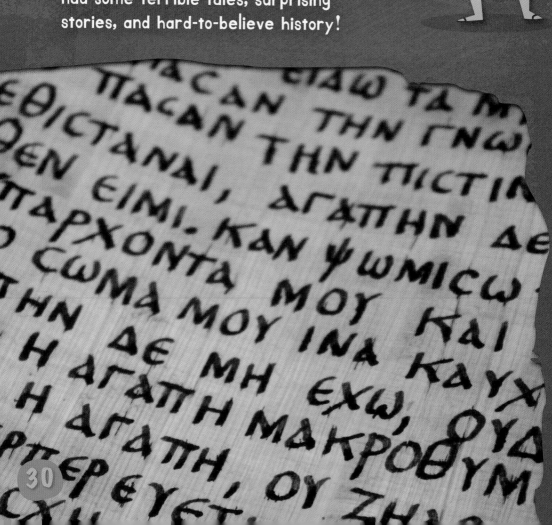

# GLOSSARY

**chariot** a two-wheeled cart pulled by horses and used for racing

**ferryman** a person whose job is to carry people across water on a boat

**fiction** something that has been imagined or made up

**gullible** easily fooled or tricked

**lead** a soft, poisonous metal

**myths** made-up stories about the distant past

**philosophers** people who seek wisdom and study how to live

**sacred** holy, or important to a religion

**shame** a painful emotion caused by guilt and embarassment

**tattoos** permanent or long-lasting marks drawn onto skin with ink

**theater** a place where people gather to perform and watch plays or listen to music or speeches

**toxic** harmful to a person's health

**tragic** very sad or upsetting

**underworld** in Greek mythology, an unpleasant place people go to after death

**venomous** able to inject poison into someone with a bite or sting

**zombies** people believed to have died and been brought back to life as monsters

# INDEX

# READ MORE

**Finan, Catherine C.** *Ancient Greece (X-treme Facts: Ancient History).* Minneapolis: Bearport Publishing Company, 2022.

**Levy, Janey.** *The Achievements of Ancient Greece (That's Ancient!).* New York: Gareth Stevens Publishing, 2022.

# LEARN MORE ONLINE

1. Go to **www.factsurfer.com** or scan the QR code below.
2. Enter **"Strange Ancient Greece"** into the search box.
3. Click on the cover of this book to see a list of websites.